Piggyback®Songs

for

Infants and Toddlers

New Songs Sung to the
Tunes of Childhood Favorites

Totline® Publications
A Division of Frank Schaffer Publications, Inc.
Torrance, California

Piggyback® Songs
for
Infants and Toddlers

Written and
Compiled by

Jean Warren

Illustrated by Marion Hopping Ekberg
Chorded by Barbara Robinson

ACKNOWLEDGEMENTS

Piggyback® is a registered trademark of Totline® Publications.

ISBN 0-911019-07-3

Library of Congress Catalog Card Number 85-050433
Edited by Elizabeth S. McKinnon
Illustrated by Marion Hopping Ekberg
Cover Design by Larry Countryman
Chorded by Barbara Robinson
Manufactured in the United States of America
Published by Totline® Publications

Business Office: 23740 Hawthorne Blvd.
Torrance, CA 90505

CONTENTS

CONTENTS

CONTENTS

CONTENTS

LULLABY SONGS

THE NIGHT-NIGHT SONG

Sung to: "Brahm's Lullaby"

     C   C   C   G7
Close your eyes, close your eyes, close your eyes and go night-night.
     G7   G7   G7   C
Close your eyes, close your eyes, close your eyes and sleep so tight.
     F   C   G7   C
Go to sleep, little toes, you've worked hard all day.
     F   C   G7   C
Go to sleep, little legs, you've run hard and played.

(Repeat first two lines.)

     F   C   G7   C
Go to sleep, little hands, you're always so busy.
     F   C   G7   C
Go to sleep, little arms, being small isn't easy.

(Repeat first two lines.)

     F   C   G7   C
Go to sleep, little ears, there's so much to hear.
     F   C   G7   C
Go to sleep, little mouth, there's nothing to fear.

(Repeat first two lines.)

Sharon Sweat
West End, NC

GO TO SLEEP

Sung to: "Silent Night"

C   C
Go to sleep, go to sleep,
G7   C
Rest your head, rest your feet.
F   C
Close your eyes and curl up tight,
F   C
Dream about the things you like.
G7   C
Sleep all though the night,
C   G7   C
Sleep till morning is light.

Jean Warren

9

LULLABY SONGS

GO TO SLEEP, LITTLE ONE

Sung to: "Frere Jacques"

C
Go to sleep,

C
Go to sleep,

C
Little one,

C
Little one.

C
When it's time to wake up,

C
You will hear the bells.

C
Ding, ding, dong.

C
Ding, ding, dong.

> Jean Warren
> Adapted Traditional

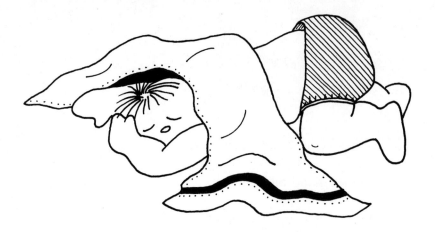

ROCK-A-BYE, BABY

G
Rock-a-bye, baby,

G   D
On the tree top.
   (Rock child in arms.)

When the wind blows,

   G
The cradle will rock.
   (Rock child in arms.)

G
When the bough breaks,

     D
The cradle will fall,
   (Let child fall a little.)

    G
And down will come baby,

D   G
Cradle and all.
   (Catch and hug child.)

> **Traditional**

SLEEPING AND WAKING SONG

Sung to: "Frere Jacques"

C   C
Close your eyes, close your eyes,

C   C
Fall asleep, dream away.

C   C
Close your eyes, fall asleep,

C   C
Little child, little child.

C   C
Fall asleep, fall asleep,

C   C
Little child, little child.

C   C
Dream away, dream away,

C   C
Fall asleep, fall asleep.

C   C
Wake up child, wake up child,

C   C
Open your eyes, open your eyes.

C   C
Time to play, time to play,

C   C
Wake up child, wake up child.

> Carolyn Arey
> Salisbury, NC

WAKE UP SONGS

WAKE UP, SLEEPY HEAD

Sung to: "Yankee Doodle"

C   C   G7
Hey, you sleepy head, wake up,
     C   G
You cannot sleep all day.
     C   F
It's time to open up your eyes
    G7   C
So you can run and play.

Frank Dally
Ankeny, IA

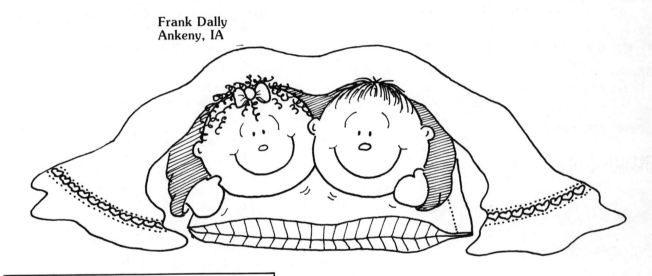

DEEDLE, DEEDLE, DUMPLING

Deedle, deedle, dumpling,

My (son/daughter) (child's name)

Went to bed with (his/her) breeches on.

One shoe off. One shoe on.

Deedle, deedle, dumpling,

My (son/daughter) (child's name).

Adapted Traditional

LITTLE ONE

Sung to: "Frere Jacques"

C   C
Are you sleeping, are you sleeping,
C   C
Little One? Little One?
C   C
Morning bells are ringing, morning bells are ringing.
C   C
Ding, ding, dong. Ding, ding, dong.

Adapted Traditional

PEEKABOO SONGS

WHERE, OH WHERE

Sung to: "The Paw Paw Patch"

C
Where, oh where, is little (child's name)?

G7
Where, oh where, is little (child's name)?

C
Where, oh where, is little (child's name)?

G7   C
(I/We) can't find (him/her) anywhere.

C
There, oh there, is little (child's name).

G7
There, oh there, is little (child's name).

C
There, oh there, is little (child's name).

G7   C
Playing peekaboo!

      Jean Warren

PEEKABOO

Sung to: "Frere Jacques"

C
Where are you hiding?

C
Where are you hiding?

C
I can't see you.

C
I can't see you.

C
Are you here or over there?

C
Are you here or over there?

C C
Peekaboo!

C C
Peekaboo!

Cover eyes with hands at the beginning of song and take away at end.

      Pat Cook
      Hartford, VT

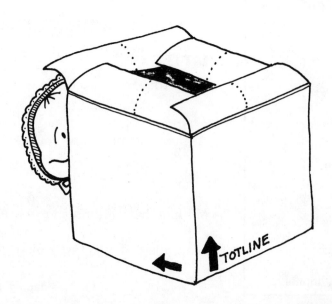

PEEKABOO SONGS

I SEE YOU

Sung to: "Frere Jacques"

C
(Child's name)'s hiding, (child's name)'s hiding,

C
Away from me, away from me.

C
Where can (he/she) be? Where can (he/she) be?

C
Peekaboo. I see you.

Jean Warren

WHERE IS BABY?

Sung to: "Frere Jacques"

C
Where is (child's name)? Where is (child's name)?

C
There (he/she) is. There (he/she) is.

C
(I'm/We're) so glad to see you. (I'm/We're) so glad to see you.

C
Peekaboo! (I/We) see you.

Jean Warren

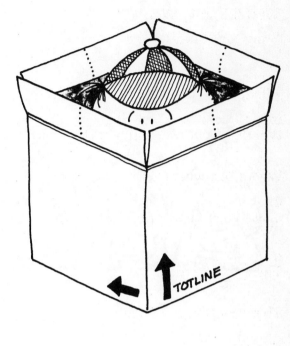

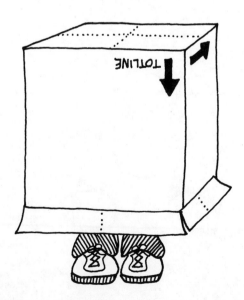

ALL AROUND THE ROOM I LOOK

Sung to: "Pop Goes the Weasel"

C   G7   C
All around the room I look,
   (Cup hands over eyes and look around room.)

 C   G7   C
I cannot find (child's name).

          C   C
Perhaps I'll look (describe where child is hiding).

F   G7   C
Boo! (He/She) was hiding!

Jean Warren

PIGGY SONGS

THIS LITTLE PIGGY

Sung to: "Frere Jacques"

    C   C
This little piggy, this little piggy,
    C   C
Went to town, went to town.
    C   C
He ran up and down, he ran up and down,
    C   C
Through the town, through the town.

    C   C
This little piggy, this little piggy,
    C   C
He stayed home, he stayed home.
    C   C
He did not like to roam, he did not like to roam,
    C   C
He stayed home, he stayed home.

Jean Warren
Adapted Traditional

TO MARKET, TO MARKET

To market, to market

To buy a fat pig.

Home again, home again,

Jiggety-jig.

To market, to market

To buy a fat hog.

Home again, home again,

Jiggety-jog.

Move child up and down on knee while
saying rhyme.

Traditional

PLAY SONGS

NAMING SONG

Sung to: "Someone's In the Kitchen With Dinah"

C
Daddy's little girl is (child's name),

C   G7
Cutest little girl he kno-o-o-ows.

C   F
Daddy's little girl is (child's name),

C   G7   C
And he loves her so.

C
Grandma's little boy is (child's name),

C   G7
Cutest little boy she kno-o-o-ows.

C   F
Grandma's little boy is (child's name),

C   G7   C
And she loves him so.

Change words to fit situation. You can also substitute a nickname for the word "girl" or "boy": "Daddy's little pumpkin, peanut, snookums, etc. is . . ."

Jean Warren

PAT-A-CAKE

Sung to: "The ABC Song"

C   C   F   C
Pat-a-cake, pat-a-cake, baker's man,

G7   C   G7   C
Bake me a cake as fast as you can.

C   G7   C   G7
Roll it and pat it and mark it with "B,"

        C   G7   C   G7
And put it in the oven for Baby and me.

C   C   F   C
Pat-a-cake, pat-a-cake, baker's man,

G7   C   G7   C
Bake me a cake as fast as you can.

Hold child's hands and act out movements.

Traditional

I CAN MAKE A BABY SMILE

Sung to: "The Muffin Man"

F   F
I can make a baby smile,

    G7   C
A baby smile, a baby smile.

F   F
I can make a baby smile

          C   F
When I tickle her on her toes.

F   F
I can make a baby laugh,

    G7   C
A baby laugh, a baby laugh.

F   F
I can make a baby laugh

          C   F
When I tickle her on her nose.

Betty Silkunas
Philadelphia, PA

GIDDY-UP SONGS

THIS IS THE WAY THE BABY RIDES

Sung to: "The Mulberry Bush"

D
This is the way the baby rides,

A7
Baby rides, baby rides.

D
This is the way the baby rides,

A7   D
Bouncy, Bouncy, Bouncy.

   (Bounce child slowly on your knee.)

D
This is the way the jockey rides,

A7
Jockey rides, jockey rides.

D
This is the way the jockey rides,

A7   D
Gallopy, Gallopy, Gallopy.

   (Bounce child faster.)

Jean Warren
Adapted Traditional

MERRY-GO-ROUND

Sung to: "This Old Man"

C   C
Merry-go-round, merry-go-round,

F   G7
We go riding all around.

C   F   C
First we're up, then we're down.

G7   C G7 C
We go riding all around.

   (Move child up and down on knee.)

C   C
Off to town, off to town,

F   G7
We go riding off to town.

C   F   C
Hold on tight, don't fall down.

   (Gently lean to one side.)

G7   C G7 C
We go riding off to town.

Jean Warren

GIDDY-UP SONGS

OLD GRAY MARE

Sung to: "Row, Row, Row Your Boat"

C   C
Clip, clip, clippety clop,
C
Clippety, clippety, clop.
   C
The old gray mare goes (up and down/round and round),
 G7   C
Until it's time to stop.

Move child up and down on knee, or walk in a circle with child on your back, while singing song.

Jean Warren

RIDE TO TOWN

Sung to: "Row, Row, Row Your Boat"

C
Ride, ride, ride to town,
C
We'll ride to town today.
C
First we'll stop and then we'll shop,
 G7   C
And then we'll ride away.

Move child up and down on knee while singing song.

Jean Warren

HIPPITY HIP, HIPPITY HOP

Sung to: "Row, Row, Row Your Boat"

C   C
Hip, hip, hippity hip,
C
Hippity, hippity, hop.
  C
We'll hop around the room today
 G7   C
Until it's time to stop.

Gently bounce child on your back and walk around room while singing song.

Jean Warren

WATCH YOU GO

Deedle, deedle, dumpling,

Ride to town,

Sometimes up, sometimes down.

Deedle, deedle, dumpling,

Watch you go,

Sometimes fast, sometimes slow.

Move child up and down on knee while saying rhyme.

Jean Warren
Adapted Traditional

BATH SONGS

SCRUB-A-DUB-DUB SONG

Sung to: "The Mulberry Bush"

C   G7
This is the way we scrub our hands, scrub our hands, scrub our hands,
C   G7   C
This is the way we scrub our hands, so early in the morning.

C   G7
This is the way we scrub our head, scrub our head, scrub our head,
C   G7   C
This is the way we scrub our head, so early in the morning.

C   G7
This is the way we scrub our elbows, scrub our elbows, scrub our elbows,
C   G7   C
This is the way we scrub our elbows, so early in the morning.

C   G7
This is the way we scrub our stomachs, scrub our stomachs, scrub our stomachs,
C   G7   C
This is the way we scrub our stomachs, so early in the morning.

Jean Warren

BATH SONGS

THIS IS THE WAY WE TAKE A BATH

Sung to: "The Mulberry Bush"

D
This is the way we take a bath,

A7
Take a bath, take a bath.

D
This is the way we take a bath,

  A7   D
So early in the morning.

D
This is the way we rub-a-dub-dub,

A7
Rub-a-dub-dub, rub-a-dub-dub.

D
This is the way we rub-a-dub-dub,

  A7   D
So early in the morning.

Additional verse: "This is the way we scrub-a-dub-dub."

Jean Warren
Adapted Traditional

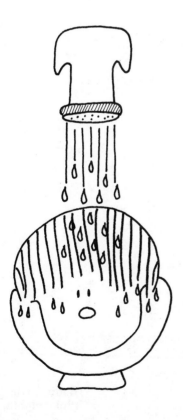

HAIR WASHING SONG

Sung to: "I'm Gonna Wash That Man Right Outa My Hair"

               F
I'm gonna wash that dirt right outa my hair,

               F
I'm gonna wash that dirt right outa my hair,

               F
I'm gonna wash that dirt right outa my hair,

  C7   F
And send it on its way.

               F
I'm gonna rinse that soap right outa my hair,

               F
I'm gonna rinse that soap right outa my hair,

               F
I'm gonna rinse that soap right outa my hair,

  C7   F
And send it on its way.

Additional verses: "I'm gonna wash that dirt right off of
my face; I'm gonna wash that dirt right off of my hands."

Sue Nydick
Philadelphia, PA

DRESSING SONGS

THIS IS THE WAY WE DRESS OURSELVES

Sung to: "The Mulberry Bush"

F
This is the way we tie our shoes,

C7   F
Tie our shoes, tie our shoes.

F   F
This is the way we tie our shoes,

   C7
So early in the morning.

Additional verses: "This is the way we pull on
our shirt; pull up our pants; put on our hat;
buckle our shoes; put on our mittens; pull on
our boots."

Betty Silkunas
Philadelphia, PA

PUT ON YOUR STOCKINGS AND SHOES

Sung to: "My Bonnie Lies Over the Ocean"

   C   F   C
It's time to put on your stockings,

   C   D7   G
It's time to put on your shoes.

   C   F   C
Sit here, sit here, little (child's name),

      F   G   C
We'll put on your stockings and shoes.

C   F
Put on, put on,

G   C
Put on your stockings and shoes.

C   F
Put on, put on,

G   C
Put on your stockings and shoes.

Elizabeth McKinnon
Seattle, WA

ALL BY MYSELF

Sung to: "Blow the Man Down"

C
All by myself

I can put on my shirt.

C   F
Push! Pull!

G7
I have it on.

G7
All by myself

I can put on my shirt.

Push! Pull!

C
I have it on.

Additional verses: "All by myself I can put
on my pants; put on my socks; tie on my
shoes."

Betty Silkunas
Philadelphia, PA

DRESSING SONGS

PUT YOUR FINGER ON YOUR SHIRT

Sung to: "If You're Happy and You Know It"

Put your finger on your shirt, [F]

On your shirt. [C]

Put your finger on your shirt,

On your shirt. [F]

Put your finger on your shirt, [Bb]

Put your finger on your shirt, [F]

Put your finger on your shirt, [C]

On your shirt. [F]

Additional verses: "Put your finger on your sweater; pants; socks; buckle; button; shoelace; belt."

Betty Silkunas
Philadelphia, PA

DRESSING SONG

Sung to: "The Farmer in the Dell"

I'm putting my blue dress on, [D]

I'm putting my blue dress on. [D]

I'm getting all dressed to look my best, [D]

I'm putting my blue dress on. [D] [A7] [D]

Repeat, using names of other items of clothing.

Elizabeth McKinnon
Seattle, WA

HEAD TO TOE SONGS

HERE'S MY ARM

Sung to: "Frere Jacques"

C   C
Here's my arm, here's my arm,
C   C
Watch me wave, watch me wave.
C
I can wave it up and down,
C
I can wave it all around.
C   C
Watch me wave, watch me wave.

C   C
Here's my leg, here's my leg,
C   C
Watch me march, watch me march.
C
I can march — up and down,
C
I can march — all around.
C   C
Watch me march, watch me march.

Continue with other body parts and movements.

Jean Warren

SHOW ME IF YOU CAN

Sung to: "In and Out the Window"

F   B♭
Whe-ere is your finger?
C   F
Whe-ere is your finger?
F   B♭
Whe-ere is your finger?
C   F
Show me if you can.

F   B♭
Good, now where's your nose?
C   F
Now, where is your nose?
F   B♭
Now, where is your nose?
C   F
Show me if you can.

Continue with other body parts.

Barbara Robinson
Glendale, AZ

HEAD TO TOE SONGS

HEAD AND SHOULDERS

Sung to: "Frere Jacques"

C   C
Head and shoulders, head and shoulders,
C   C
Knees and toes, knees and toes.
C
Head and shoulders, head and shoulders,
C
Knees and toes, knees and toes.

C   C
Eyes and ears, eyes and ears,
C   C
Mouth and nose, mouth and nose.
C
Eyes and ears, eyes and ears,
C
Mouth and nose, mouth and nose.

Traditional

A FLY IS ON MY NOSE

Sung to: "The Farmer in the Dell"

  C
A fly is on my nose,
  C
A fly is on my nose.
   C
Heigh-ho, just watch me blow,
  C   G7   C
A fly is on my nose.

Additional verses: "A fly is on my head; ear;
elbow; toe; knee;" etc.

Jean Warren

TAP YOUR HEAD

Tap your head.

Tap your toe.

Turn in a circle.

Bend down low.

Tap your nose.

Tap your knees.

Hands on your shoulders.

Sit down, please.

Margery Kranyik
Hyde Park, MA

WIGGLE YOUR TOES

Sung to: "Row, Row, Row Your Boat"

C
Wiggle, wiggle, wiggle your toes,
C
Wiggle them up and down.
C
Wiggle them fast, wiggle them slow,
G7   C
Wiggle them all around.

Additional verses: "Wave, wave, wave your
arm; Stomp, stomp, stomp your foot; Blink,
blink, blink your eyes."

Jean Warren

HEAD TO TOE SONGS

PUT YOUR FINGER ON YOUR NOSE

Sung to: "If You're Happy and You Know It"

      C   G7
Put your finger on your nose, on your nose,
     G7   C
Put your finger on your nose, on your nose.
     F
Put your finger on your nose, and feel it as it grows,
     G7   C
Put your finger on your nose, on your nose.

      C   G7
Put your finger on your toe, on your toe,
     G7   C
Put your finger on your toe, on your toe.
     F   C
Put your finger on your toe, and move it to and fro,
     G7   C
Put your finger on your toe, on your toe.

      C   G7
Put your finger on your ear, on your ear,
     G7   C
Put your finger on your ear, on your ear.
     F   C
Put your finger on your ear, and see if it's still here,
     G7   C
Put your finger on your ear, on your ear.

Make up other verses about different body parts.

Jean Warren

EENY, MEENY, MINEY, MO

Sung to: "This Old Man"

C   C
Eeny, meeny, miney, mo,
F   G7
Catch (child's name) by the toe.
    C   F   C
And if (he/she) hollers let (him/her) go.
G7   C   G7 C
Eeny, meeny, miney, mo.

Adapted Traditional

MY TOE IS STARTING TO MOVE

Sung to: "The Bear Went Over the Mountain"

    C   F   C
My toe is starting to move,
    G7   C
My toe is starting to move,
    C   F
My toe is starting to move,
C   G7   C
As I first wake up.

    C   F   C
My leg is starting to move,
    G7   C
My leg is starting to move,
    C   F
My leg is starting to move,
C   G7   C
As I first wake up.

Continue with other body parts until whole body
is up and moving.

Jean Warren

HEAD TO TOE SONGS

NICK NACK PADDY WACK

Sung to: "This Old Man"

C
This old man was a spy,
F   G7
He played nick nack on my eye.
       C   F
With a nick nack paddy wack
C
Give a dog a bone,
G7   C G7   C
This old man came rolling home.

    (Additional verses)

C
This old man liked to doze,
F   G7
He played nick nack on my nose.

C
This old man lived down south,
F   G7
He played nick nack on my mouth.

C
This old man couldn't hear,
F   G7
He played nick nack on my ear.

C
This old man liked to linger,
F   G7
He played nick nack on my finger.

C
This old man went to the farm,
F   G7
He played nick nack on my arm.

C
This old man kicked a keg,
F   G7
He played nick nack on my leg.

Susan Nydick
Philadelphia, PA

Adapted Traditional

HERE WE GO LOOBY LOO

C
Here we go looby loo,
               G7
Here we go looby light.
C
Here we go looby loo,
G7   C
All on a Saturday night.

     C
You put a hand in,
     C
You take a hand out.
      C
You give your hand a shake, shake, shake,
     C G7   C
And turn yourself about.

Repeat chorus and second verse using "a foot;
your head; whole self."

Adapted Traditional

25

FINGER SONGS

IF YOUR CLOTHES HAVE ANY RED

Sung to: "If You're Happy and You Know It"

C   G7
If your clothes have any red, any red,

G7   C
If your clothes have any red, any red.

F   C
If your clothes have any red, put your finger on your head,

G7   C
If your clothes have any red, any red.

C   G7
If your clothes have any blue, any blue,

G7   C
If your clothes have any blue, any blue.

F   C
If your clothes have any blue, put your finger on your shoe,

G7   C
If your clothes have any blue, any blue.

Additional verses: "If your clothes have any green, wave your hand so you are seen; If your clothes have any yellow, smile like a happy fellow; If your clothes have any brown, turn your smile into a frown; If your clothes have any black, put your hands behind your back."

Jean Warren
Adapted Traditional

MY FINGERS

Sung to: "The Mulberry Bush"

F
This is the way my fingers play,

C
Fingers play, fingers play.

F
This is the way my fingers play,

C   F
So early in the morning.

Additional verses: "This is the way my fingers march; dance; run; wave; sleep."

Jean Warren

FINGER RHYMES

OPEN, SHUT THEM

Open, shut them,

Open, shut them,

Let your hands go "clap."

Open, shut them,

Open, shut them,

Put them on your lap.

Creep them, creep them,

Creep them, creep them,

Right up to your chin.

Open up your little mouth,

But do not let them in!

Say the last line quickly, then pretend
to bite down hard.

Traditional

TEN LITTLE FINGERS

I have ten little fingers,

And they all belong to me.

I can make them do things.

Would you like to see?

I can put them up high,

I can put them down low,

I can make them hide,

And I can fold them, so.

Traditional

KNOCK, KNOCK

Knock, knock.
   (Knock on child's forehead.)

Peek in.
   (Cup hands around your eyes.)

Open the latch.
   (Push on child's nose.)

And walk right in.
   (Walk fingers into child's mouth.)

Traditional

I WIGGLE

I wiggle, wiggle, wiggle my fingers,

I wiggle, wiggle, wiggle my toes.

I wiggle, wiggle, wiggle my shoulders,

I wiggle, wiggle, wiggle my nose.

Now no more wiggles are left in me,

So I will be as still as can be.

Traditional

27

LOVE SONGS

HUG ME, HUG ME, HUG ME

Sung to: "Music, Music, Music"

C
All I want are hugs from you,
C
Hugs that last the whole day through,
D7   G7
Hugs just make me feel so good,
    C
So hug me, hug me, hug me.

G7   C
Hug me, so things won't bug me,
         G7
So I can smile and smile the whole day through,
C7   Edim Dm   G
Smile until I'm back with you.

      C
So give me lots of hugs today,
C
Hugs that chase the blues away,
D7   G7
Hugs that last the whole day through,
      C   C
So hug me, hug me, hug me.

Jean Warren

I LOVE YOU

Sung to: "This Old Man"

C
I Love You, I Love You.
F   G7
Je T'Aime means I Love You.
C   F   C
Oh yes, oh yes, oh y-es I do.
G7   C G7   C
Je T'Aime means I Love You.

Repeat, using the Spanish "Yo Te Amo"
and the German "Ich Liebe Dich."

Jean Warren

BEST FRIENDS

Sung to: "Frere Jacques"

C   C
We are special, we are special,
C   C
Look at us, look at us.
C   C
We are best friends, we are best friends,
C   C
Yes we are, yes we are!

Carolyn Arey
Salisbury, NC

28

SPECIAL SONGS

BIG OR LITTLE SONG

Sung to: "In and Out the Window"

Adult sings:

C   G
How big are you today?
G   C
How big are you today?
C   G
How big are you today?
G   C
Show me with your hands.

Child replies with adult's help:

C   G
I'm oh, so very big,
G   C
I'm oh, so very big,
C   G
I'm oh, so very big.
G   C
Just watch me as I grow.

(Child stretches out hands farther and farther.)

Adult sings:

C   G
How small are you today?
G   C
How small are you today?
C   G
How small are you today?
G   C
Show me if you can.

Child replies with adult's help:

C   G
I can grow so very little,
G   C
I can grow so very little,
C   G
I can grow so very little.
G   C
Just watch me grow so small.

(Child squats down farther and farther
and curls up into a tiny ball.)

Jean Warren

HAPPY BIRTHDAY, TWO'S AND THREE'S

Sung to: "Skip to My Lou"

F
It's (child's name)'s birthday, toodly doo,
C7
It's (child's name)'s birthday, toodly doo,
F
It's (child's name)'s birthday, toodly doo,
C7   F
Oh, so big! Now (he's/she's) two!

F
(Child's name) had a birthday, yes siree,
C7
(Child's name) had a birthday, yes siree,
F
(Child's name) had a birthday, yes siree,
C7   F
(He's/She's) so big! (He/She) is three!

Jean Warren

29

WELCOME SONGS

HELLO SONG

Sung to: "London Bridge"

C
Everybody smile and wave,

G7   C
Smile and wave, smile and wave.

C
Everybody smile and wave.

G7   C
Here comes (child's name).

C
Everybody say hello,

G7   C
Say hello, say hello.

C
Everybody say hello.

G7   C
Hello, (child's name).

Jean Warren

WELCOME

Sung to: "Twinkle, Twinkle, Little Star"

C   F   C
Welcome, welcome, everyone,

G7   C   G7   C
Now you're here, we'll have some fun.

C   G7   C   G7
First we'll clap our hands just so,

C   G7   C   G7
Then we'll bend and touch our toe.

C   C   F   C
Welcome, welcome, everyone,

G7   C   G7   C
Now you're here, we'll have some fun.

Jean Warren

30

WELCOME SONGS

OH, HERE WE ARE TOGETHER

Sung to: "Did You Ever See A Lassie?"

     F   C   F
Oh, here we are together, together, together,

     F   C   F
Oh, here we are together, how happy are we.

          C   F   C   F
There's (child's name) and (child's name) and (child's name) and (child's name),

     F   C   F
Oh, here we are together, so happy are we.

Traditional

MARY WORE HER RED DRESS

Sung to: "Did You Ever See a Lassie?"

F   C   F
Mary wore her red dress, her red dress, her red dress,

F   C   F
Mary wore her red dress to school today.

F   C   F
Johnny wore his green jeans, his green jeans, his green jeans,

F   C   F
Johnny wore his green jeans to school today.

Pick out something pretty or nice about each child's clothing and then sing about it. You might also ask the children what they have on that they would like everyone to sing about.

Traditional

WELCOME SONGS

COME, LET'S SING

Sung to: "This Old Man"

C
Come, let's sing — Song One,
     G7
We can sing it just for fun.
      C   F   C
With a do, re, mi, fa, sol, la, ti, do,
G7   C G7 C
Let's all sing as we go.

C
Come, let's sing — Song Two,
      G7
I will sing it just for you.
      C   F   C
With a do, re, mi, fa, sol, la, ti, do,
G7   C G7 C
Let's all sing as we go.

C
Come, let's sing — Song Three,
      G7
You can sing it just for me.
      C   F   C
With a do, re, mi, fa, sol, la, ti, do,
G7   C G7 C
Let's all sing as we go.

C
Come, let's sing — Song Four,
      G7
We can sing it out the door.
      C   F   C
With a do, re, mi, fa, sol, la, ti, do,
G7   C G7 C
Let's all sing as we go.

Jean Warren

I AM SO HAPPY

Sung to: "You Are My Sunshine"

              F
I am so happy, so very happy,
F7   B♭   F
I want to sing all day long.
   F7   B♭   F
I am so happy, so very happy,
                   C7   F
Won't you come and sing along?

Let children sing about why they are happy.
Examples: "I am so happy because it's Easter; I am
so happy I have new shoes; I am so happy the sun
is shining;" etc.

Jean Warren

IF YOU'RE HAPPY AND YOU KNOW IT

         F
If you're happy and you know it,
              C
Clap your hands.
              C
If you're happy and you know it,
         F
Clap your hands.
              B♭
If you're happy and you know it,
              F
Then your face will surely show it.
              C
If you're happy and you know it,
         F
Clap your hands.

Traditional

GOODBYE SONGS

OH, IT'S TIME TO SAY GOODBYE

Sung to: "She'll Be Coming Round the Mountain"

    F
Oh, it's time to say goodbye to our friends,
    F   C7
Oh, it's time to say goodbye to our friends.
    F
Oh, it's time to say goodbye,
    B^b
Make a smile and wink an eye.
    F   C7   F
Oh, it's time to say goodbye to our friends.

Additional verse: "Oh, it's time to wave goodbye to
our friends."

Jean Warren

THANK YOU SONG

Sung to: "London Bridge"

C
Merci means Thank You,
G7   C
Thank You, Thank You.
C
Merci means Thank You.
G7 C
I Thank You.

Repeat, using the German "Danka," the Spanish
"Gracias," and the Japanese "Arigato."

Jean Warren

WE ARE HELPING

Sung to: "London Bridge"

C
Who will put the _____ away,
G7   C
_____ away, _____ away?
C
Who will put the _____ away?
G7   C
Who is helping?

Use words such as "blocks, cars, toys," etc. in the blanks.

C
Put the _____ on the shelf,
G7   C
On the shelf, on the shelf.
C
Put the _____ on the shelf.
G7   C
We are helping.

Use words such as "puzzles, crayons, paper," etc. in the
blanks.

Frank Dally
Ankeny, IA

MOVEMENT SONGS

LET'S GO WALKING

Sung to: "Frere Jacques"

C   C
Let's go walking, let's go walking.
C   C
Walk, walk, walk. Walk, walk, walk.
C   C
Now we are hopping, now we are hopping.
C   C
Hop, hop, hop. Hop, hop, hop.

C   C
Now we are running, now we are running.
C   C
Run, run, run. Run, run, run.
C   C
Now we are stopping, now we are stopping.
C   C
Stop, stop, stop. Stop, stop, stop.

Jean Warren

COME ON NOW

Sung to: "Ten Little Indians"

C   C
Come on now, let's go walking,
G7   G7
Come on now, stop your talking.
C   C
Come on now, let's go walking,
G7   C
All around the (room/yard).

C   C
Come on (child's name), let's go walking,
G7   G7
Come on (child's name), stop your talking.
C   C
Come on (child's name), let's go walking,
G7   C
All around the (room/yard).

Repeat, using other children's names. Have each
child take hold of the hand of the last person called,
forming a single line. Continue until everyone is in
line.

Jean Warren

34

MOVEMENT SONGS

MAGIC FEET

Sung to: "The Muffin Man"

C   C
Have you seen my magic feet,
F   G7
Dancing down the magic street?
C   C
Sometimes fast, sometimes slow,
G7   C
Sometimes high, sometimes low.

C   C
Come and dance along with me,
F   G7
Dance just like my feet you see.
C   C
First we'll slide and then we'll hop,
G7   C
Then we'll spin and then we'll stop.

Jean Warren

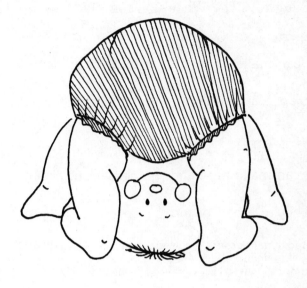

AROUND THE BLOCK

Sung to: "Frere Jacques"

C   C
Let's go walking, let's go walking,
C   C
Around the block, around the block.
C   C
We will keep on walking, we will keep on walking.
C   C
Then we'll stop. Then we'll stop.

Additional verses: "Let's go running; skipping; marching; hopping;" etc.

Jean Warren

GOING TO TOWN

Sung to: "Skip to My Lou"

F
Going to town, two by two,
C7
Going to town, two by two.
F
Going to town, two by two,
C7   F
Skip to my Lou, my darling.

F
Everyone's welcome, come along too,
C7
Everyone's welcome, come along too.
F
Everyone's welcome, come along too,
C7   F
Skip to my Lou, my darling.

Change "town" to whatever location you are headed. For example: "the playground; the lunch room; the music room;" etc.

Jean Warren

35

MOVEMENT SONGS

THEY'RE A PART OF ME

Sung to: "The Wheels on the Bus"

F
I can make my hands go clap, clap, clap,
C
Clap, clap, clap,
F
Clap, clap, clap.
F
I can make my hands go clap, clap, clap.
C   F
They're a part of me.

Additional verses: "I can make my *eyes* go
blink; fingers go snap; feet go stomp; legs go
jump; tongue go click; hips go wiggle; lips go
kiss."

                          Frank Dally
                          Ankeny, IA

DID YOU EVER SEE A JUMPING BEAN?

Sung to: "Did You Ever See a Lassie?"

          C
Did you ever see a jumping bean,
  G   C
A jumping bean, a jumping bean?
          C
Did you ever see a jumping bean
  G   C
Jump this way and that?
  G   C
Jump this way and that way,
  G   C
Jump this way and that way.
          C   C
Did you ever see a jumping bean
  G   C
Jump this way and that?

                    Saundra Winnett
                    Fort Worth, TX

SEE ME SWINGING

Sung to: "Frere Jacques"

C   C
See me swinging, see me swinging,
C   C
Oh, so high, oh, so high.
C   C
Higher and higher, higher and higher.
C   C
Touch the sky, touch the sky.

                    Saundra Winnett
                    Fort Worth, TX

WE CAN DO

Sung to: "The Mulberry Bush"

F
We can do what Jenny does,
C7   F
Jenny does, Jenny does.
F
We can do what Jenny does,
C7   F
And we're going to do it now.

Let "Jenny" make a movement and have the
children copy it. Then repeat the song for the
next child.

                    Frank Dally
                    Ankeny, IA

36

MOVEMENT SONGS

HAPPILY WE SKIP ALONG

Sung to: "Merrily We Roll Along"

F
Happily we skip along,
C   F
Skip along, skip along.
F
Happily we skip along,
C   F
As we sing this song.

Additional verses: "Proudly we march
along; Sleepily we walk along; Slowly we
crawl along; Merrily we run along;" etc.

Jean Warren

CATCH THE POPCORN IF YOU CAN

Sung to: "This Old Man"

C
Watch me pop in the pan.
F   G7
Try to catch me if you can,
     C   F   C
While I hop and pop and jump to and fro.
G7   C G7 C
Try to catch me as I go.

As a second verse, have the children sing just
the word "pop" as they hop around the room.

Jean Warren

RUN LIKE I DO

Sung to: "Oh, My Darling Clementine"

         F   F
Run like I do, run like I do,
         F   C
Run like I am doing now.
         C   F
Run like I do, run like I do,
         C   F
Run like I am doing now.

Repeat, substituting these words for "run":
"skip, march, hop, jump, crawl, wave," etc.

Jean Warren

CLAP YOUR HANDS

Sung to: "Row, Row, Row Your Boat"

C
Clap, clap, clap your hands,
C
Clap them all around.
C   C
Clap them loud, then clap them soft,
   G7   C
Now, don't make a sound.

C
Stamp, stamp, stamp your feet,
C
Stamp them all around.
C   C
Stamp them loud, then stamp them soft,
   G7   C
Now, don't make a sound.

Jean Warren

DANCE SONGS

COME AND DANCE

Sung to: "Who's Afraid of the Big Bad Wolf?"

C   G7
Come and dance around with me,

G7   C
Round with me, round with me.

C   G7
Come and dance around with me,

G7   C
Tra - la - la - la - la.

C   G7
First we'll skip around the room,

G7   C
Round the room, round the room.

C   G7
First we'll skip around the room,

G7   C
Tra - la - la - la -la.

C   G7
Then we'll sway to and fro,

G7   C
To and fro, to and fro.

C   G7
Then we'll sway to and fro,

G7   C
Tra - la - la - la - la.

C   G7
Now we'll spin around and round,

G7   C
Around and round, around and round.

C   G7
Now we'll spin around and round,

G7   C
Tra - la - la - la -la.

C   G7
All join hands and circle round,

G7   C
Circle round, circle round.

C   G7
All join hands and circle round,

G7   C
Tra - la - la - la - la.

Jean Warren

DANCE SONGS

I LIKE TO DANCE

Sung to: "Skip to My Lou"

F
I like to dance, how about you?
C7
I like to dance, how about you?
F
I like to dance, how about you?
C7   F
Skip to my Lou, my darling.

Let children each choose a movement
and lead the song. For example: "I like
to skip; run; march; swing;" etc.

Jean Warren

LITTLE SHADOW

Sung to: "Skip to My Lou"

F
Dance, dance, just like me,
C7
Dance, dance, just like me.
F
Dance, dance, just like me,
C7   F
Little shadow, just like me.

Additional verses: "Raise your hand, just
like me; Kick your foot, just like me; Bend
way down, just like me; Flap your arms, just
like me," etc.

Jean Warren

DANCE, DANCE

Sung to: "Ten Little Indians"

C   C
Dance, dance, little (child's name),
G7   G7
Dance, dance, little (child's name),
C   C
Dance, dance, little (child's name),
G7   C
While (I/we) sing this song.

C   C
Turn, turn, little (child's name),
G7   G7
Turn, turn, little (child's name),
C   C
Turn, turn, little (child's name),
G7   C
While (I/we) sing this song.

C   C
Clap, clap, little (child's name),
G7   G7
Clap, clap, little (child's name),
C   C
Clap, clap, little (child's name),
G7   C
While (I/we) sing this song.

For group participation, change wording to:
"Dance, dance, everyone; Turn, turn, everyone; Clap, clap, everyone."

Jean Warren

RHYTHM SONGS

TAP YOUR STICKS

Sung to: "The Paw Paw Patch"

F
Tap, tap, tap your sticks,
C
Tap, tap, tap your sticks,
F
Tap, tap, tap your sticks,
C   F
While we march around the room.

F
High, high, tap them high,
C
Low, low, tap them low,
F
Fast, fast, tap them fast,
C   F
Now let's al-l tap them slow.

   (Sing last line slowly.)

Additional verses: "Ring your bells; Tap your drums."

Jean Warren

LET'S ALL TAP OUR BELLS

Sung to: "The Mulberry Bush"

D
Let's all tap our bells today,
A7
Bells today, bells today.
D
Let's all tap our bells today,
A7   D
Let's tap them on our hand.

Repeat, using "Let's tap them on our
elbow, foot, arm, head," etc. This also
could be used to sing about rhythm sticks
or drums: "Let's all tap our sticks today;
Let's all beat our drums today."

Jean Warren

RING YOUR BELL

Sung to: "If You're Happy and You Know It"

          C   G7
Ring your bell in the air, in the air,
          G7   C
Ring your bell in the air, in the air.
          F
Ring your bell in the air,
       C
For no one will care.
          G7   C
Ring your bell in the air, in the air.

          C   G7
Ring your bell on your hand, on your hand,
          G7   C
Ring your bell on your hand, on your hand.
          F
Ring your bell on your hand,
       C
Then everybody stand.
          G7   C
Ring your bell on your hand, on your hand.

This also could be sung using other rhythm instruments.
For example: "Tap your sticks; Beat your drum;" etc.

Jean Warren

BELL SONGS

JINGLE ALL THE WAY

Sung to: "Jingle Bells"

C   C
Jingle bells, jingle bells,
C
Jingle all the way.
G7   C
Oh, what fun it is to play
      G
My jingle bells today-a.

C   C
Shake them fast, shake them slow,
C
Shake them loud and clear.
G7   C
Oh, what fun it is to shake
     G7   C
When Christmas time is near.

Jean Warren
Adapted Traditional

HEAR THE BELLS

Sung to: "The ABC Song"

C   F   C
One, two, three, four, five, six, seven,
G7   C G7   C
Hear the bells up in heaven.
C   F   C   G7
Eight, nine, ten, eleven, twelve,
C   G7   C G7   C
Ring them soft, then ring them loud.

Jean Warren

ARE YOU LISTENING?

Sung to: "Frere Jacques"

C   C
Are you listening, are you listening,
C   C
Brother John? Brother John?
C
Christmas bells are ringing.
C
Christmas bells are ringing.
C   C
Ding, ding, dong. Ding, ding, dong.

Adapted Traditional

LITTLE BELL

Sung to: "This Old Man"

C
Little bell, little bell,
F   G7
If I ask you, will you tell-l
C   F   C
Why you always se-em to-o chime
G7   C G7   C
When it's close to Christmas time?

Jean Warren

MARCHING SONGS

NUMBER MARCH, ONE TO FIVE

Sung to: "Skip to My Lou"

F
Marching together, one by one,
C7
Marching together, one by one,
F
Marching together, one by one.
C7   F
Marching together — Oh what fun!

    (Children march in a circle.)

F
Marching together, two by two,
C7
Marching together, two by two,
F
Marching together, two by two.
C7   F
You march with me — I'll march with you.

    (Children march in groups of two.)

F
Marching together, three by three,
C7
Marching together, three by three,
F
Marching together, three by three.
C7   F
Marching together — Look at me!

    (Children march in groups of three.)

F
Marching together, four by four,
C7
Marching together, four by four,
F
Marching together, four by four.
C7   F
Marching together — Let's march some more.

    (Children march in groups of four.)

F
Marching together, five by five,
C7
Marching together, five by five,
F
Marching together, five by five,
C7   F
No more children will arrive.

    (Children march in groups of five.)

Betty Ruth Baker
Waco, TX

MARCHING SONGS

HEAR THEM PLAY

Sung to: "Frere Jacques"

C   C
See the drums, see the drums,
C   C
Hear them play, hear them play.
C   C
Rat-a-tat-a-tat-tat, Rat-a-tat-a-tat-tat,
C   C
Hear them play, hear them play.

C   C
See the horns, see the horns,
C   C
Hear them play, hear them play.
C   C
Root-a-toot-a-toot-toot, Root-a-toot-a-toot-toot,
C   C
Hear them play, hear them play.

C   C
See the bells, see the bells,
C   C
Hear them play, hear them play.
C   C
Ring-a-ling-a-ling-ling, Ring-a-ling-a-ling-ling,
C   C
Hear them play, hear them play.

Jean Warren

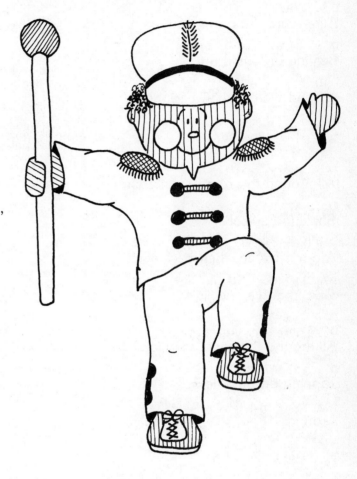

MARCHING BAND

Sung to: "I'm a Little Teapot"

C   F   C
Marching down the street is so much fun.
G7   C   G7   C
Watch the band. Here we come.
C   F   C
When we march together, hear us play.
F   C   G7   C
We're a marching band today.

Jean Warren

MARCH ALONG

Sung to: "This Old Man"

C   C
March along, march along,
F   G
Lift your feet up off the ground.
         C   C
And we'll march and sing a happy little song,
G   C   G   C
As we go a marching on.

Diana Nazaruk
Clark Lake, MI

MARCHING SONGS

ALL AROUND THE ROOM WE MARCH

Sung to: "Pop Goes the Weasel" (first stanza)

D   A7
All around the room we march,

D   A7   D
Beating on our drum.

    D   A7   D
Around we go, then back again.

A7   D
Gee, that was fun!

D   A7   D
All around the room we march,

D   A7   D
Shaking our bell.

    D   A7   D
Around we go, then back again.

A7   D
Gee, that was swell!

D   A7   D
All around the room we march,

D   A7   D
Tapping on our sticks.

    D   A7   D
Around we go, then back again.

A7   D
Gee, what kicks!

Jean Warren

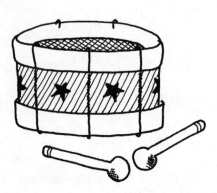

LET'S ALL MARCH DOWN THE STREET

Sung to: "If You're Happy and You Know It"

         C   G7
Let's all march down the street, down the street,

         G7   C
Let's all march down the street, down the street.

         F
Let's all march down the street,

             C
Smile at everyone we meet.

         G   C
Let's all march down the street, down the street.

Repeat, using "skip, run, crawl, hop," etc.

Jean Warren

MARCHING SONG

Sung to: "The Bear Went Over the Mountain"

         F   B♭   F
We marched over the mountain,

         C   F
We marched over the mountain.

         C   Bb
We marched over the mountain,

         F   C   F
And what do you think we saw?

         F   B♭   F
We saw another mountain,

         C   F
We saw another mountain.

         F   B♭
We saw another mountain,

         F   C   F
And what do you think we did?

Repeat.

Adapted Traditional

TRAVELING SONGS

OUT TO SEA

Sung to: "Row, Row, Row Your Boat"

C
Row, row, row your boat,

C
Row it out to sea.

C
The more you row, the farther you go,

     G7   C
And the more that you will see.

Jean Warren

WAGON RIDE

Sung to: "The Paw Paw Patch"

F
Hop aboard my (red/blue/green) wagon,

C
Hop aboard my (red/blue/green) wagon,

F
Hop aboard my (red/blue/green) wagon,

C   F
Then we'll ride around the (room/yard/block).

F
Round, round, round we go,

C
Round, round, round we go,

F
Round, round, round we go,

C   F
All around the (room/yard/block).

Jean Warren

OVER THE RIVER

C
Over the river and through the woods

    F   C
To Grandmother's house we go.

    Dm   G7
The horse knows the way

    C   Am
To carry the sleigh

             D7   G   G7
Through the white and drifted snow — oh,

C
Over the river and through the woods

    F   C
Oh, how the wind does blow.

    F   B7   C   Am
It stings the nose and bites the toes

    C   G7   C
As over the ground we go.

Traditional

TRAVELING SONGS

OLD MACDONALD'S TRUCK

Sung to: "Old MacDonald Had a Farm"

F   B♭   F   F C F
Old MacDonald had a truck, E-I-E-I-O.
    F   B♭   F   F C F
And into town he drove his truck, E-I-E-I-O.

       F
With a bump, bump here,

       F
And a bump, bump there,
F   F
Here a bump, there a bump,

F
Everywhere a bump, bump.
F   B♭   F   F C F
Old MacDonald had a truck, E-I-E-I-O.

F   B♭   F   F C F
Old MacDonald had a truck, E-I-E-I-O.
    F   B♭   F C F
And on his truck he had a horn, E-I-E-I-O.

     F
With a beep, beep here,

     F
And a beep, beep there,
F   F
Here a beep, there a beep,

F
Everywhere a beep, beep.
F   B♭   F   F C F
Old MacDonald had a truck, E-I-E-I-O.

Adapted Traditional

I'M A WINDSHIELD WIPER

Sung to: "I'm a Little Teapot"

C
I'm a windshield wiper,
F   C
Watch me wipe

G7   C
First on the left side,
G7   C
Then on the right.

C
I just love to wipe

         F   C
And wipe and wipe.

C   F   G7   C
I can wipe all day and night.

Jean Warren

TRAVELING SONGS

THE WHEELS ON THE BUS

          F   F
Oh, the wheels on the bus go round and round,

C   F
Round and round, round and round.

          F   F
Oh, the wheels on the bus go round and round,

C   F
All through the town.

    (Make circling motions with hands.)

          F   F
Oh, the wipers on the bus go swish, swish, swish,

C   F
Swish, swish, swish; swish, swish, swish.

          F   F
Oh, the wipers on the bus go swish, swish, swish,

C   F
All through the town.

    (Move hands back and forth like windshield wipers.)

          F   F
Oh, the people on the bus go up and down,

C   F
Up and down, up and down.

          F   F
Oh, the people on the bus go up and down,

C   F
All through the town.

    (Move body up and down.)

Additional verses: "The horn on the bus goes 'toot, toot, toot';
The baby on the bus goes 'waa, waa, waa'; The mother on the
bus goes 'shh, shh, shh';" etc.

Traditional

LET'S GO DRIVING

Sung to: "Frere Jacques"

C   C
Let's go driving, let's go driving,

C   C
Around the block, around the block.

C   C
We will keep on driving, we will keep on driving,

C   C
Then we'll stop, then we'll stop.

Jean Warren

CAR SONGS

RIDING IN THE CAR

Sung to: "The Farmer in the Dell"

       F
We're riding in the car,

       F
We're riding in the car.

F
Heigh-ho, away we go,

       F   C   F
We're riding in the car.

       F
We're riding oh, so far,

       F
We're riding oh, so far.

F
Heigh-ho, away we go,

       F   C   F
We're riding in the car.

Jean Warren

DRIVING SONG

Sung to: "She'll Be Coming Round the Mountain"

       F
(She'll/He'll) be driving a new car when (she/he) comes,

       F   C7
(She'll/He'll) be driving a new car when (she/he) comes.

       F
(She'll/He'll) be driving a new car,

       Bᵇ
(She'll/He'll) be driving a new car,

       F   C7   F
(She'll/He'll) be driving a new car when (she/he) comes.

Make up other verses such as: "He'll be driving a Mack truck when he comes; I'll be driving my new camper when I come;" etc.

Jean Warren

WHAT'S ON IT?

Sung to: "Old MacDonald Had a Farm"

F   Bᵇ   F   F C F
(Child's name) had a car, E-I-E-I-O.

       F   Bᵇ   F   F C F
And on this car (he/she) had some wheels, E-I-E-I-O.

           F
With a wheel here,

           F
And a wheel there,

F   F
Here a wheel, there a wheel,

F
Everywhere a wheel, wheel.

F   Bᵇ   F   F C F
(Child's name) had a car, E-I-E-I-O.

Repeat, letting child help name vehicle and what is on it: "bus - doors; truck - windows; train - cars;" etc.

Jean Warren

48

CAR SONGS

LOOKING OUT THE WINDOW

Sung to: "In and Out the Window"

F   C
Let's look out the window,

C   F
Let's look out the window,

F   B^b
Let's look out the window,

      C   F
And see what we can see.

    F   C
I see a   (adjective)   (noun) ,

    C   F
I see a _____ _____ ,

    F   B^b
I see a _____ _____ ,

    C   F
And that is what I see.

Repeat second verse letting child sing about different things he or she sees.

Jean Warren
Adapted Traditional

WATCHING THE WORLD GO BY

Sung to: "My Bonnie Lies Over the Ocean"

    F   B^b F
I love to ride in a car,

F   B^b C
Now I will tell you why.

    F   B^b F
I love to look out the window,

      B^b C   F
And watch the cars go by.

F   B^b
Cars, cars, cars, cars,

C   F
Just watch the cars go by, go by.

F   B^b
Cars, cars, cars, cars,

C   F
Just watch the cars go by.

Repeat, substituting words such as these for the word "car": "bus, truck, plane, van, helicopter." Let your children decide what they want to watch.

Jean Warren

TRAIN SONGS

LITTLE RED TRAIN

Sung to: "Row, Row, Row Your Boat"

C
Here comes the Little Red Train,
C
Chugging down the track.
  C
It first goes down, then turns around,
G7   C
Then it chugs right back.

C
See it hook on cars,
C
Chugging as it goes.
    C
The Little Red Train never stops,
G7   C
It just grows and grows.

Jean Warren

CLICKETY-CLACK

Clickety-clack, clickety-clack,

See the train

On the track.

Clickety-clack, clickety-clack,

See the train

Going back.

Let the children pretend they are trains going forward and backward on the tracks.

Adapted Traditional

TRAIN SONGS

I'M A LITTLE RED TRAIN

Sung to: "I'm a Little White Duck"

      F
I'm a little red train

          C
Chugging down the track,

 C
A little red train

       F
Going up and back.

 F
I travel all day

       C
Going round and round,

C   F
Taking goods from town to town.

    F
I'm a little red train

      C
Going down the track,

C   F
Chug — Chug — Chug.

Jean Warren

DOWN BY THE STATION

C
Down by the station

G7   C
Early in the morning,

C
See the little pufferbillies

G7   C
All in a row.

C
See the station master

G7   C
Pull a little handle.

C
Chug, chug. Toot, toot.

G7   C
Off we go!

Traditional

51

ANIMAL SONGS

LITTLE PUPPY

Sung to: "Twinkle, Twinkle, Little Star"

C   F   C
Little puppy, happy and gay,

G7   C   G7   C
Won't you please come out to play?

    G7   C   G7
Lick my face and wag your tail,

C   G7   C   G7
We'll have fun that will not fail.

C   F   C
Little puppy, happy and gay,

G7   C   G7   C
Won't you please come out to play?

Betty Silkunas
Philadelphia, PA

I'M A LITTLE KITTEN

Sung to: "I'm a Little Teapot"

C
I'm a little kitten,

F   C
Soft and furry.

G7   C
I will be your friend,

   G7   C
So don't you worry.

C   F   C
Right up on your lap I like to hop.

F   C
Purr, purr, purr,

   G7   C
And never stop.

Betty Silkunas
Philadelphia, PA

MY KITTEN

Sung to: "Sing a Song of Sixpence"

  C
I have a little kitten,

      G
She's black and white and gray.

G7
When I try to cuddle her,

      C
She always wants to play.

C
So I drag a piece of yarn

        F
Across the kitchen floor.

      G
She thinks it is a little mouse,

         C
And always asks for more.

Elizabeth Vollrath
Stevens Point, WI

52

ANIMAL SONGS

THE MOUSE RAN AROUND THE ROOM

Sung to: "The Bear Went Over the Mountain"

    C   F   C
The mouse ran around the room,
   (Make circling motions with arms.)
    G   C
The mouse ran around the room,
    C   F
The mouse ran around the room,
      G   C
And what do you think he saw?
    C   F   C
He saw a great big cat,
   (Raise arms and make a large circle.)
    C   F   C
He saw a great big cat,
    C   F   C
He saw a great big cat,
    C   F   G7
So what do you think he did?
   (Repeat verse until you are tired.)

    C   F C
The mouse ran into his hole,
   (Squat down.)
    G7   C
The mouse ran into his hole,
    C   F
The mouse ran into his hole,
C   G7   C
Safe and sound at last.
   (Cover head with arms.)

            Jean Warren

HICKORY, DICKORY, DOCK

Hickory, dickory, dock.

The mouse ran up the clock.

The clock struck one,

The mouse ran down.

Hickory, dickory, dock.

Traditional

ANIMAL SONGS

TWO LITTLE BLACKBIRDS
Sung to: "Frere Jacques"

C   C
Two little blackbirds, two little blackbirds,
   (Hold up two pointer fingers.)
C   C
Sitting on a hill, sitting on a hill.
   (Make a hill with both hands.)
C   C
One named Jack, one named Jack,
   (Hold up one pointer finger.)
C   C
One named Jill, one named Jill.
   (Hold up other pointer finger.)

C   C
Two little blackbirds, two little blackbirds,
   (Hold up two pointer fingers.)
C   C
Flew away, flew away.
   (Move both hands behind back.)
C   C
Jack flew back, Jack flew back,
   (Bring out one hand, pointer finger raised.)
C   C
Then came Jill, then came Jill.
   (Bring out other hand, pointer finger raised.)

Adapted Traditional

SHOO, FLY

Shoo, fly, don't bother me,

Shoo, fly, don't bother me.

Shoo, fly, don't bother me,

For I have work to do.

Child pretends to bat away fly while saying verse.

Adapted Traditional

ALL AROUND THE YARD
Sung to: "Ten Little Indians"

C
Craw, crawl, little snake,
G7
Crawl, crawl, little snake.
C
Crawl, crawl, little snake,
G7   C
All around the yard.

Additional verses: "Wiggle, wiggle, little worm; Buzz, buzz, little bee; Fly, fly, butterfly; Run, run, little bug."

Jean Warren

ANIMAL SONGS

I WISH I WERE A BUNNY

Sung to: "Did You Ever See a Lassie?"

  F   F
I wish I were a bunny,
   C   F
A bunny, a bunny.
  F   F
I wish I were a bunny,
        C   F
'Cause bunnies can hop.

     C   F
They hop, and hop,
     C   F
And hop, and hop.

     F   F
Oh, I wish I were a bunny,
        C   F
'Cause bunnies can hop.

Additional verses: "I wish I were a horse, 'cause horses can gallop; I wish I were a frog, 'cause froggies can jump; I wish I were a fish, 'cause fishes can swim."

Jean Warren

SEE THE BUG

Sung to: "Frere Jacques"

C   C
See the bug, see the bug,
C   C
Watch him crawl, watch him crawl.
C   C
See him crawling higher, see him crawling higher,
C   C
Watch him crawl, up the wall.

C   C
See the bug, see the bug,
C   C
Watch him go, watch him go.
C   C
See him crawling lower, see him crawling lower,
C   C
Way down low, to my toe.

C   C
See the bug, see the bug,
C   C
Watch him grin, watch him grin.
C   C
See him crawling higher, see him crawling higher,
C   C
To my chin, to my chin.

Jean Warren

BUMBLE BEE SONGS

BUMBLE BEE ON MY NOSE

Sung to: "Jingle Bells"

C   C
Bumble Bee, Bumble Bee,
C   C
Landing on my toes.
G7   C
Bumble Bee, Bumble Bee,
G7
Now he's on my nose.

C   C
On my arms, on my legs,
C
On my elbows.
G7   C
Bumble Bee, oh, Bumble Bee,
   G7   C
He lands and then he goes.

Jean Warren

BUMBLE BEE, BUMBLE BEE

Bumble Bee, Bumble Bee,

Buzzing all around.

Bumble Bee, Bumble Bee,

Buzzing on the ground.

> (Pinch fingers together to repre-
> sent bee and make buzzing sound.)

Bumble Bee, Bumble Bee,

Buzzing up so high.

Bumble Bee, Bumble Bee,

Buzzing in the sky.

Bumble Bee, Bumble Bee,

Buzzing past your toes.

Bumble Bee, Bumble Bee,

Buzzing on your nose.

> (Have bee fly around and land
> on child's nose.)

Jean Warren

BUMBLE BEE SONGS

BUZZING ROUND THE ROOM

Sung to: "When Johnny Comes Marching Home Again"

   Em
A bee is buzzing round the room,

    G
Buzz buzz, buzz buzz.

   Em
A bee is buzzing round the room,

    B
Buzz buzz, buzz buzz.

   G   D
He'll buzz around the room once more,

     Em   B
And then he'll buzz right out the door.

       Em Am Em B
And we'll all be glad when

Em   Am   Em
He is gone once more.

Jean Warren

BUMBLE BEE

Sung to: "Robin Hood"

F   C   B^b F
Bumble Bee, Bumble Bee,

G7   C
Flying through the air.

F   C   B^b F
Bumble Bee, Bumble Bee,

G7   C
Landing in my hair.

F   C
What should I do?

B^b F
I'm so-o scared!

F   C   F
Bumble Bee, Bumble Bee, Bumble Bee!

Jean Warren

BARNYARD SONGS

BAA, BAA, BLACK SHEEP

Sung to: "Twinkle, Twinkle, Little Star"

C
Baa, baa, black sheep,

F   C
Have you any wool?

G7   C
Yes, sir, yes, sir,

G7   C
Three bags full.

C   G7
One for my master,

     C   G7
And one for the dame,

     C   G7
And one for the little boy

      C   G7
Who lives down the lane.

C
Baa, baa, black sheep,

F   C
Have you any wool?

G7   C
Yes, sir, yes, sir,

G7   C
Three bags full.

Adapted Traditional

OLD MACDONALD HAD A FARM

F B^b F   F   C   F
Old MacDonald had a farm, E-I-E-I-O.

            F B^b F   F   C   F
And on his farm he had a pig, E-I-E-I-O.

              F   F
With an oink, oink here, and an oink, oink there,

F   F   F
Here an oink, there an oink, everywhere an oink, oink.

F B^b F   F   C   F
Old MacDonald had a farm, E-I-E-I-O.

           F B^b F   F   C   F
And on his farm he had a cow, E-I-E-I-O.

            F   F
With a moo, moo here, and a moo, moo there,

F   F
Here a moo, there a moo, everywhere a moo, moo.

F B^b F   F   C   F
Old MacDonald had a farm, E-I-E-I-O.

Continue, letting children suggest names of other animals.

Traditional

BARNYARD SONGS

OVER IN THE BARNYARD

Sung to: "Down By the Station"

C
Over in the barnyard
G7   C
Early in the morning,
C   C
See the little duckies
G7   C
Standing in a row.
C
See the busy farmer
G7   C
Giving them their breakfast.
C
Quack, quack, quack, quack.
G7   C
Off they go.

Repeat, using other barnyard animal names
and sounds.

                           Jean Warren

ALL AROUND THE BARNYARD

Sung to: "Ten Little Indians"

C
Waddle, waddle, little duck,
G7
Waddle, waddle, little duck.
C
Waddle, waddle, little duck,
G7   C
All around the barnyard.

Additional verses: "Gallop, gallop little pony;
Peck, peck, little chicken; Hop, hop, little
bunny."

                           Jean Warren

LITTLE BOY BLUE

Sung to: "Twinkle, Twinkle, Little Star"

C   F   C
Little Boy Blue, come blow your horn,
(Pretend to blow horn.)
     G7   C   G7   C
The sheep's in the meadow, the cow's in the corn.
(Gesture with hands to the right and to the left.)
C   G7   C   G7
Where's the boy who looks after the sheep?
(Cup hand over eyes and look around.)
C   G7   C G7
He's under the haystack, fast asleep.
(Pretend to fall asleep.)
C   F   C
Little Boy Blue, come blow your horn,
(Pretend to blow horn.)
     G7   C   G7   C
The sheep's in the meadow, the cow's in the corn.
(Gesture with hands to the right and to the left.)

                           Adapted Traditional

ZOO SONGS

THE ZOO

Sung to: "Skip To My Lou"

F   F
Come along children, we're going to the zoo,
C7   C7
Come along children, we're going to the zoo,
F   F
Come along children, we're going to the zoo.
C7   F
Going to the zoo today.

F   F
See the animals living in the zoo,
C7   C7
See the animals living in the zoo,
F   F
See the animals living in the zoo.
C7   F
Living in the zoo today.

F   F
I see a monkey sitting in a tree,
C7   C7
I see a monkey sitting in a tree,
F   F
I see a monkey sitting in a tree.
C7   F
I see a monkey and it sees me.

F   F
I see an elephant, big and gray,
C7   C7
I see an elephant, big and gray,
F   F
I see an elephant, big and gray.
C7   F
Big gray elephant is eating hay.

F   F
I see a lion in a cage,
C7   C7
I see a lion in a cage,
F   F
I see a lion in a cage.
C7   F   F
I see a lion that roars with rage.

F   F
I see a camel with a great big hump,
C7   C7
I see a camel with a great big hump,
F   F
I see a camel with a great big hump.
C7   F   F
When he walks he goes "bump, bump."

F   F
I see a zebra, black and white,
C7   C7
I see a zebra, black and white,
F   F
I see a zebra, black and white.
C7   F
Seeing the zebra is a sight.

F   F
I see a giraffe, big and tall,
C7   C7
I see a giraffe, big and tall,
F   F
I see a giraffe, big and tall.
C7   F
He's not hard to see at all.

F   F
We saw the animals living in the zoo,
C7   C7
We saw the animals living in the zoo,
F   F
We saw the animals living in the zoo.
C7   F
Living in the zoo today.

Betty Ruth Baker
Waco, TX

ZOO SONGS

THE ELEPHANT

Sung to: "The Mulberry Bush"

    D
The elephant goes like this and that,
A7
This and that, this and that.
    (Walk heavily and stomp feet.)
    D
The elephant goes like this and that,
     A7   D
Cause he's so big and he's so fat.
    (Puff up cheeks and stretch out arms.)

    D
He has no fingers and has no toes,
A7
Has no fingers and has no toes.
    (Wiggle fingers; wiggle toes.)
    D
He has no fingers and has no toes,
    A7   D
But goodness, gracious, what a nose!
    (Pull hands out from face to suggest long trunk.)

Adapted Traditional

UNDERNEATH THE MONKEY TREE

Sung to: "The Muffin Man"

G
Come and play awhile with me,
C   D7
Underneath the monkey tree.
G
Monkey See and Monkey Do,
D7   G
Just like monkeys in the zoo.
    (Join hands and move in a circle.)

G
Swing your tail, one, two, three,
C   D7
Underneath the monkey tree.
G
Monkey See and Monkey Do,
D7   G
Just like monkeys in the zoo.
    (Put hands behind back and pretend to swing tail.)

G
Jump around and smile like me,
C   D7
Underneath the monkey tree.
G
Monkey See and Monkey Do,
D7   G
Just like monkeys in the zoo.
    (Jump and smile.)

Jean Warren

FALL SONGS

TWO LITTLE APPLES

Sung to: "This Old Man"

C   C
Way up high, in a tree,
>   (Raise arms high over head.)

F   G7
Two red apples smiled at me.
>   (Smile.)

      C   F   C
So I shook that tree as har-r-d as I could.
>   (Pretend to shake tree.)

G7   C   G7   C
Down came the apples. Ummm, they were good!
>   (Rub tummy.)

>   Jean Warren
>   Adapted Traditional

WITCHES COME ON HALLOWEEN

Sung to: "Camptown Races"

F
Witches come on Halloween,
C
Heh-heh, Heh-heh!
F
Watch out now or you might scream,
C   F
Heh, heh, heh, heh, heh!
F
Pumpkins shining bright,
B♭   F
With their candlelight.
F
Ghosts and goblins coming too,
C   F   F
Watching out for you—BOO!

>   Judy Hall
>   Wytheville, VA

PUMPKIN, PUMPKIN

Pumpkin, Pumpkin,

Sitting on the wall.
>   (Child sits on floor.)

Pumpkin, Pumpkin,

Tip and fall.
>   (Child tips and falls over.)

Pumpkin, Pumpkin,

Rolling down the street.
>   (Child rolls on floor.)

Pumpkin, Pumpkin,

Trick-or Treat.

Traditional

FALL SONGS

LITTLE SPIDER

See the little Spider

Climbing up the wall.
   (Crawl fingers slowly up child's arm.)

See the little Spider

Stumble and fall.
   (Crawl fingers quickly down child's arm.

See the little Spider

Tumble down the street.
   (Crawl fingers down child's leg.)

See the little Spider

Stop down at your feet.
   (Stop fingers at child's feet.)

Traditional

TEENY, TINY SPIDER

Sung to: "Eensy, Weensy Spider"

F
Teeny, tiny spider

      C   F
Climbed under a big bridge.
   (Sitting on floor, child moves wiggling hand under raised knees.)

F
Down came the bridge

      C   F
And knocked the spider out.
   (Child brings knees down on hand.)

F
Up went the bridge,
   (Child raises knees.)

      C   F
And never again

      F   F
Did the teeny, tiny spider

   C   F
Go under a big bridge.
   (Child moves wiggling hand out from under knees.)

Jean Warren

SPIN, SPIN, LITTLE SPIDER

Sung to: "Ten Little Indians"

C
Spin, spin, little spider,

G7
Spin, spin, wider, wider.

C
Spin, spin, little spider,

G7   C
Early in the morning.

C
Dance, dance, little spider,

G7
Dance, dance, dance out wider.

C
Dance, dance, little spider,

G7   C
Early in the morning.

Repeat second verse using these words: "jump, crawl, run."

Jean Warren

FALL SONGS

THANKSGIVING SONG

Sung to: "The Farmer in the Dell"

     F   F
The turkey says gobble,
     F   F
The turkey says gobble.
F   F
Heigh-ho on Thanksgiving,
     F   C   F
The turkey says gobble.

Linda Blum
Scotia, New York

GOBBLE, GOBBLE, TURKEY

Gobble, Gobble, Turkey,

Running all around.

Gobble, Gobble, Turkey,

Falling to the ground.

Gobble, Gobble, Turkey,

Standing up so straight.

Gobble, Gobble, Turkey,

Running through the gate.

Traditional

MY TURKEY

I have a turkey, big and fat.

He spreads his wings
   (Fan hands at hips.)

And walks like that.
   (Strut.)

His daily corn he would not miss,
   (Pretend to eat corn.)

And when he talks, he sounds like this!
   ("Gobble, gobble, gobble.")

Dee Hoffman and Juda Panko
Aitkin, MN

WINTER SONGS

HERE STANDS A
LOVELY CHRISTMAS TREE

Sung to: "The Mulberry Bush"

D
Here stands a lovely Christmas tree,

A
Christmas tree, Christmas tree.

D
Here stands a lovely Christmas tree,

  A7   D
So early in the morning.

    (Hold hands over head, fingers touching.)

D
Here is a horn for the Christmas tree,

A7
Christmas tree, Christmas tree,

D
Here is a horn for the Christmas tree,

  A7   D
So early in the morning.

    (Hold hands to mouth and blow.)

D
Here is a drum for the Christmas tree,

A7
Christmas tree, Christmas tree.

D
Here is a drum for the Christmas tree,

  A7   D
So early in the morning.

    (Pretend to beat drum.)

D
Here are the lights for the Christmas tree,

A
Christmas tree, Christmas tree.

D
Here are the lights for the Christmas tree,

  A7   D
So early in the morning.

    (Flutter fingers.)

D
Here stands a lovely Christmas tree,

A
Christmas tree, Christmas tree.

D
Here stands a lovely Christmas tree,

  A7   D
So early in the morning.

    (Hold hands over head, fingers touching.)

Traditional

WINTER SONGS

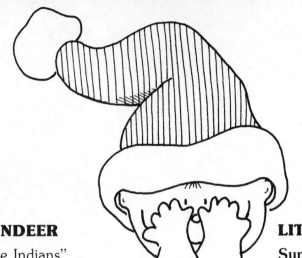

TEN LITTLE REINDEER

Sung to: "Ten Little Indians"

F   F
One little, two little, three little reindeer,
C   C
Four little, five little, six little reindeer,
F   F
Seven little, eight little, nine little reindeer,
C   F
Pulling Santa's sleigh.

Mrs. Gary McNitt
Adrian, MI

LITTLE STAR

Sung to: "Music, Music, Music"

F
Twinkle, twinkle, little star,
F
Twinkle, twinkle, out so far.
G7   C7
All you do the whole night through
   F
Is twinkle, twinkle, twinkle.

Flutter fingers while singing song.

Jean Warren

I'VE SEEN A SANTA

I've seen a Santa, jolly and fat.
   (Hold hands in a circle at waist.)

He strokes his beard
   (Pretend to stroke beard.)

And laughs like that.
   ("Ho, Ho, Ho.")

He puts his pack into his sleigh
   (Pretend to put pack in sleigh.)

All loaded with toys.

Let's shout, "Hooray!"

Dee Hoffman and Juda Panko
Aitkin, MN

CHRISTMAS EVE

When Santa fills my stocking,
   (Pretend to fill stocking.)

I wish that I could peek.
   (Peek through fingers.)

But Santa never, ever comes
   (Shake head.)

Till I am fast asleep.
   (Pretend to fall asleep.)

Traditional

WINTER SONGS

SNOWFLAKES IN MY HAIR

Sung to: "On the Good Ship Lollipop"

     C
There are snowflakes in my hair,
     G7
There are snowflakes everywhere.

So sing with me

         C
'Bout the snowflakes th-at we can see.

Additional verses: "There is sunshine; There are raindrops."

Jean Warren

I'M A LITTLE VALENTINE

Sung to: "I'm a Little Teapot"

C
I'm a little Valentine,
F   **C**
Red and white.
F   **C**
With ribbons and lace,
   G7   **C**
I'm a beautiful sight.

C
I can say, "I love you,"
  F   **C**
On Valentine's Day.
   F   **C**
Just put me in an envelope
  G7   **C**
And give me away!

Vicki Claybrook
Kennewick, WA

PLEASE BE MY VALENTINE

Sung to: "The Farmer in the Dell"

       F
Please be my Valentine,
       F
Please be my Valentine.
F
I'll be yours if you'll be mine,
       F   **C** **F**
Please be my Valentine.

Elizabeth McKinnon
Seattle, WA

SPRING SONGS

I'M THE EASTER BUNNY

Sung to: "I'm a Little Teapot"

C   F   C
I'm the Easter Bunny, soft and white.

G7   C   G7   C
Here are my ears and tail so light.

    (Put one hand above head, two fingers raised,
    to make ears, and one hand behind back, fist
    closed to make tail.)

C   F   C
Hiding Easter eggs all over town,

      F   C   G7   C
Now watch me hop, hop all around.

    (Hop like a bunny.)

Judy Hall
Wytheville, VA

EASTER BUNNY

Sung to: "Mary Had a Little Lamb"

C
Easter Bunny by the tree,

G7   C
By the tree, by the tree.

C
Easter Bunny by the tree,

G7   C
Won't you come and play with me?

C
Easter Bunny hop around,

G7   C
Hop around, hop around.

C
Easter Bunny hop around,

G   C
Place your eggs upon the ground.

Jean Warren

HERE IS A BUNNY

Sung to: "The Mulberry Bush"

D
Here is a bunny with ears so funny,

A7
Ears so funny, ears so funny.

    (Wiggle two fingers up behind your head.)

D
Here is a bunny with ears so funny,

    A7   D
And here is his hole in the ground.

    (Put your hand on your hip, creating a "hole.")

     D
He pricks up his ears when a noise he hears,

A7
Noise he hears, noise he hears.

    (Straighten your fingers.)

     D
He pricks up his ears when a noise he hears,

    A7   D
And jumps in his hole in the ground.

    (Put your hand in "hole.")

Adapted Traditional

SPRING SONGS

PLANTING TIME

Sung to: "Row, Row, Row Your Boat"

C
Dig, dig, dig the earth,

    (Make digging motion.)

C
Then you plant your seeds.

    (Pretend to drop seeds.)

   C
A gentle rain

    (Flutter fingers down.)

And bright sunshine

    (Circle arms above head.)

   G7   C
Will help your flowers grow.

    (Hold one arm parallel to ground
    and move other arm up behind it
    with fingers extended to repre-
    sent a flower growing.)

                  Vicki Claybrook
                  Kennewick, WA

IT'S RAINING, IT'S POURING

      C   C
It's raining, it's pouring,

       C   C
The old man is snoring.

   G7
He went to bed and bumped his head,

   G7   C
And couldn't get up in the morning.

              Traditional

FOR YOU, MAMA

Sung to: "Frere Jacques"

C   C
For you, Mamma, for you, Mama,

C   C
I love you, I love you.

C   C
I made a present, I made a present,

C   C
Just for you, just for you.

                Saundra Winnett
                Fort Worth, TX

SUMMER SONGS

OH, RING AROUND THE SUN

Sung to: "The Farmer in the Dell"

F
Oh, ring around the sun.

F
Oh, ring around the moon.

F
Oh ring around our great big world,

F   C   F
While we sing this tune.

          Jean Warren

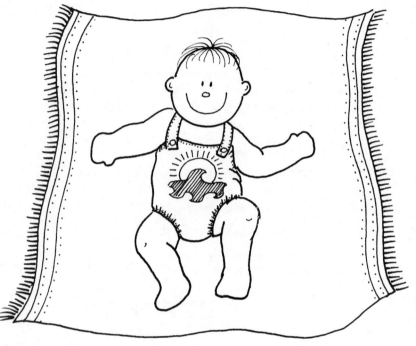

BRIGHT SUN

Sung to: "Row, Row, Row Your Boat"

C
Bright sun shining down,

   (Spread fingers and move hands down slowly.)

C
Shining on the ground.

C
What a lovely face you have,

   (Make a large circle in front of face with arms.)

G7   C
Yellow, big and round.

         Susan A. Miller
         Kutztown, PA

I'M A FISH

Sung to: "I'm a Little Teapot"

G   C   G
I'm a little fishy, I can swim.

C   G D   G
Here is my tail, here is my fin.

G   C   G
When I want to have fun with my friend,

  C   G   D   G
I wiggle my tail and dive right in.

         Lynn Beaird
         Loma Linda, CA

SUMMER SONGS

HELLO BUBBLE

Sung to: "Frere Jacques"

C   C
Hello Bubble, Hello Bubble,
C   C
Come and land, come and land.
C   C
Right in the middle, right in the middle
C   C
Of my hand, of my hand.

> (Flutter fingers of one hand down onto out-
> stretched palm of other hand.)

C   C
Goodbye Bubble, Goodbye Bubble,
C   C
Time to go, time to go.
C   C
I will help you, I will help you
C   C
With a blow, with a blow.

> (Pretend to blow bubble off hand.)

Additional verses: "Hello Feather; Hello Ladybug;
Hello Butterfly;" etc.

Jean Warren

I HEAR THUNDER

Sung to: "Frere Jacques"

C   C
I hear thunder, I hear thunder.
C   C
Do you, too? Do you, too?
C   C
Pitter-patter raindrops, pitter-patter raindrops.
C   C
I'm wet through. So are you.

Adapted Traditional

COUNTING SONGS

I CAN COUNT

Sung to: "Frere Jacques"

c
I can count,
c
I can count,
c
One, two, three,
c
One, two, three.
c
I can count higher,
c
I can count higher,
c
Four, five, six,
c
Four, five, six.

c
I can count,
c
I can count,
c
One, two, three,
c
Four, five, six.
c
I can count higher,
c
I can count higher,
c
Seven, eight, nine,
c
Seven, eight, nine.

Continue, adding higher numbers as learned.

Saundra Winnett
Fort Worth, TX

ONE, TWO, THREE

Sung to: "Frere Jacques"

c   c
One, two, three, one, two, three,
c   c
Sing with me, sing with me.
c   c
One, two, three, one, two, three,
c   c
Sing with me, sing with me.

c   c
Four, five, six, four, five, six,
c   c
Sing with me, sing with me.
c   c
Four, five, six, four, five, six,
c   c
Sing with me, sing with me.

Continue, counting on up to twelve. You can also use letters of the alphabet instead of numbers when singing this song.

Jean Warren

ONE POTATO, TWO POTATO

One potato, two potato

Three potato, four.

Five potato, six potato,

Seven potato, more.

Traditional

72

COUNTING SONGS

CLAP ONE, TWO, THREE

Sung to: "Row, Row, Row Your Boat"

C
Clap, clap, clap your hands,
C
Clap them one, two, three.
    C
The more you clap, the more we count,
  G7   C
So what will your count be?

C
One, two, three, four,
C
Five, six, seven.
    C
The more you clap, the more we count,
G7   C
Eight, nine, ten, eleven.

Adapted Traditional

FOUR RED APPLES

Sung to: "This Old Man"

C   C
Four red apples on the tree,
F   G7
Two for you and two for me.
C F   C
So-o shake that tree and watch them fall,
G7   C G7 C
One, two, three, four. That is all.

Jean Warren

HOT CROSS BUNS

Hot cross buns!

Hot cross buns!

One a penny,

Two a penny,

Hot cross buns!

Traditional

OLD TIME FAVORITES

HUMPTY DUMPTY

Sung to: "Twinkle, Twinkle, Little Star"

C   F   C
Humpty Dumpty sat on a wall,
   (Squat down.)

G7   C   G7   C
Humpty Dumpty had a great fall.
   (Roll over onto floor.)

C   F   C   G7
All the King's horses and all the King's men

C   F   C   G7
Couldn't put Humpty together again.

C   F   C
Humpty Dumpty sat on a wall,
   (Resume squatting position.)

G7   C   F   G7   C
Humpty Dumpty had a great fall.
   (Roll over onto floor.)

Adapted Traditional

JACK BE NIMBLE

Jack be nimble,

Jack be quick.

Jack jump over

The candlestick.

Traditional

LITTLE BO-PEEP

Sung to: "Jack and Jill Went Up the Hill"

C   G
Little Bo-peep has lost her sheep

       C   G7 C
And doesn't know where to find them.
   (Cup hand over eyes and look around.)

F   C   G
Leave them alone, and they'll come home,

F   C   G7 C
Wagging their tails behind them.
   (Put hands behind back and pretend to wag tail.)

Adapted Traditional

74

OLD TIME FAVORITES

WHERE IS THUMBKIN?

Sung to: "Frere Jacques"

C
Where is Thumbkin?

   (Hide one hand behind back.)

C
Where is Thumbkin?

   (Hide other hand behind back.)

C
Here I am!

   (Bring one fist forward and lift thumb.)

C
Here I am!

   (Bring other fist forward and lift thumb.)

C
How are you today, sir?

   (Move one thumb up and down as if bowing.)

C
Very well, I thank you.

   (Move other thumb up and down as if bowing.)

C
Run away.

   (Wiggling thumb, put one fist behind back.)

C
Run away.

   (Wiggling thumb, put other fist behind back.)

                Traditional

JACK-IN-THE-BOX

Jack-in-the-box, you sit so still.

   (Close hand with thumb inside.)

Won't you come out? Yes, I will!

   (Pop out thumb.)

          Traditional

MY BALLOON

Sung to: "Pop Goes the Weasel" (first stanza)

C   G7   C
Here I have a big balloon,

C   G7   C
Watch me while I blow.

C   G7   C
Small at first, then bigger,

   (Make circle with thumbs and fingers.)

G7   C
Watch it grow and grow.

   (Make bigger and bigger circles with arms.)

C   G7   C
Do you think it's big enough?

C   G7   C
Maybe I should stop.

   C G7   C
For if I blow much longer,

G7   C
My balloon will pop!

          Adapted Traditional

OLD TIME FAVORITES

I'M A LITTLE TEAPOT

C
I'm a little teapot,
F   C
Short and stout.
G7   C
Here is my handle,
    (Put hand on hip.)
G7   C
Here is my spout.
    (Extend opposite arm sideways, hand out.)

C   C
When I get all steamed up,
F   C
Then I shout,
F
"Tip me over
      C   G7 C
And pour me out!"
    (Tip sideways, "spout" side.)

C
I'm a very clever pot,
F
It is true.
G7   C
Here's an example
    G7   C
Of what I can do.

C
I can change my handle
     F   C
And change my spout.
    (Change position of hands.)
     F
Just tip me over
     G7   C
And pour me out.
    (Tip sideways, "spout" side.)

Traditional

TALL AS A TREE

Tall as a tree.
    (Raise arms high over head.)

High as a house.
    (Stretch arms out wide.)

Thin as a pin.
    (Hold arms next to body.)

Small as a mouse.
    (Huddle down in squatting position.)

Traditional

TEDDY BEAR SONGS

TEN LITTLE TEDDY BEARS

Sung to: "Ten Little Indians"

C
One little, two little, three little Teddy Bears,
G7
Four little, five little, six little Teddy Bears,
C
Seven little, eight little, nine little Teddy Bears,
G7   C
Ten little Teddy Bears.

> **Mary Evelyn Barcus**
> **Indianapolis, IN**

TEDDY BEAR, TEDDY BEAR

Teddy Bear, Teddy Bear,

Turn around.

Teddy Bear, Teddy Bear,

Touch the ground.

Teddy Bear, Teddy Bear,

Reach up high.

Teddy Bear, Teddy Bear,

Touch the sky.

Teddy Bear, Teddy Bear,

Bend down low.

Teddy Bear, Teddy Bear,

Touch your toe.

Adapted Traditional

DID YOU EVER SEE A TEDDY BEAR?

Sung to: "Did You Ever See a Lassie?"

          C
Did you ever see a Teddy Bear,
   G7   C
A Teddy Bear, a Teddy Bear?
             C
Did you ever see a Teddy Bear
   G7   C
Go this way and that?
   G7   C
Go this way and that way,
      G7   C
And this way and that way.
             C
Did you ever see a Teddy Bear
   G7   C
Go this way and that?

> **Mary Evelyn Barcus**
> **Indianapolis, IN**

77

TITLE INDEX

TITLE INDEX

Totline® PUBLICATIONS

Teacher Resources

ART SERIES
Ideas for successful art experiences.
Cooperative Art
Special Day Art
Outdoor Art

BEST OF TOTLINE® SERIES
Totline's best ideas.
Best of Totline Newsletter
Best of Totline Bear Hugs
Best of Totline Parent Flyers

BUSY BEES SERIES
Seasonal ideas for twos and threes.
Fall • Winter • Spring • Summer

CELEBRATIONS SERIES
Early learning through celebrations.
Small World Celebrations
Special Day Celebrations
Great Big Holiday Celebrations
Celebrating Likes and Differences

CIRCLE TIME SERIES
Put the spotlight on circle time!
Introducing Concepts at Circle Time
Music and Dramatics at Circle Time
Storytime Ideas for Circle Time

EMPOWERING KIDS SERIES
Positive solutions to behavior issues.
Can-Do Kids
Problem-Solving Kids

EXPLORING SERIES
Versatile, hands-on learning.
Exploring Sand • Exploring Water

FOUR SEASONS
Active learning through the year.
Art • Math • Movement • Science

JUST RIGHT PATTERNS
8-page, reproducible pattern folders.
Valentine's Day • St. Patrick's Day •
Easter • Halloween • Thanksgiving •
Hanukkah • Christmas • Kwanzaa •
Spring • Summer • Autumn •
Winter • Air Transportation • Land
Transportation • Service Vehicles
• Water Transportation • Train
• Desert Life • Farm Life • Forest
Life • Ocean Life • Wetland Life
• Zoo Life • Prehistoric Life

KINDERSTATION SERIES
Learning centers for kindergarten.
Calculation Station
Communication Station
Creation Station
Investigation Station

1•2•3 SERIES
Open-ended learning.
Art • Blocks • Games • Colors •
Puppets • Reading & Writing •
Math • Science • Shapes

1001 SERIES
Super reference books.
1001 Teaching Props
1001 Teaching Tips
1001 Rhymes & Fingerplays

PIGGYBACK® SONG BOOKS
New lyrics sung to favorite tunes!
Piggyback Songs
More Piggyback Songs
Piggyback Songs for Infants
and Toddlers
Holiday Piggyback Songs
Animal Piggyback Songs
Piggyback Songs for School
Piggyback Songs to Sign
Spanish Piggyback Songs
More Piggyback Songs for School

PROJECT BOOK SERIES
*Reproducible, cross-curricular project
books and project ideas.*
Start With Art
Start With Science

REPRODUCIBLE RHYMES
*Make-and-take-home books for
emergent readers.*
Alphabet Rhymes • Object Rhymes

SNACKS SERIES
Nutrition combines with learning.
Super Snacks • Healthy Snacks •
Teaching Snacks • Multicultural Snacks

TERRIFIC TIPS
Handy resources with valuable ideas.
Terrific Tips for Directors
Terrific Tips for Toddler Teachers
Terrific Tips for Preschool Teachers

THEME-A-SAURUS® SERIES
Classroom-tested, instant themes.
Theme-A-Saurus
Theme-A-Saurus II
Toddler Theme-A-Saurus
Alphabet Theme-A-Saurus
Nursery Rhyme Theme-A-Saurus
Storytime Theme-A-Saurus
Multisensory Theme-A-Saurus
Transportation Theme-A-Saurus
Field Trip Theme-A-Saurus

TODDLER RESOURCES
Great for working with 18 mos–3 yrs.
Playtime Props for Toddlers
Toddler Art

Parent Resources

A YEAR OF FUN SERIES
Age-specific books for parenting.
Just for Babies • Just for Ones •
Just for Twos • Just for Threes •
Just for Fours • Just for Fives

LEARN WITH PIGGYBACK® SONGS
*Captivating music with
age-appropriate themes.*
Songs & Games for…
Babies • Toddlers • Threes • Fours
Sing a Song of…
Letters • Animals • Colors • Holidays
• Me • Nature • Numbers

LEARN WITH STICKERS
*Beginning workbook and first reader
with 100-plus stickers.*
Balloons • Birds • Bows • Bugs •
Butterflies • Buttons • Eggs • Flags •
Flowers • Hearts • Leaves • Mittens

MY FIRST COLORING BOOK
*White illustrations on black back-
grounds—perfect for toddlers!*
All About Colors
All About Numbers
Under the Sea
Over and Under
Party Animals
Tops and Bottoms

PLAY AND LEARN
Activities for learning through play.
Blocks • Instruments • Kitchen
Gadgets • Paper • Puppets • Puzzles

RAINY DAY FUN
*This activity book for parent-child fun
keeps minds active on rainy days!*

RHYME & REASON STICKER WORKBOOKS
*Sticker fun to boost
language development and
thinking skills.*
Up in Space
All About Weather
At the Zoo
On the Farm
Things That Go
Under the Sea

SEEDS FOR SUCCESS
*Ideas to help children develop
essential life skills for future success.*
Growing Creative Kids
Growing Happy Kids
Growing Responsible Kids
Growing Thinking Kids

THEME CALENDARS
Activities for every day.
Toddler Theme Calendar
Preschool Theme Calendar
Kindergarten Theme Calendar

TIME TO LEARN
Ideas for hands-on learning.
Colors • Letters • Measuring •
Numbers • Science • Shapes •
Matching and Sorting • New Words
• Cutting and Pasting •
Drawing and Writing • Listening •
Taking Care of Myself

Posters
Celebrating Childhood Posters
Reminder Posters

Puppet Pals
Instant puppets!
Children's Favorites • The Three Bears
• Nursery Rhymes • Old MacDonald
• More Nursery Rhymes • Three
Little Pigs • Three Billy Goats Gruff •
Little Red Riding Hood

Manipulatives

CIRCLE PUZZLES
African Adventure Puzzle

LITTLE BUILDER STACKING CARDS
Castle • The Three Little Pigs

Tot-Mobiles
*Each set includes four punch-out,
easy-to-assemble mobiles.*
Animals & Toys
Beginning Concepts
Four Seasons

**Start right,
start bright!**

Totline products are available at parent and teacher stores.